U.S.A. TRAVEL GUIDES

WASHINGTON

BY ANN HEINRICHS • ILLUSTRATED BY MATT KANIA

The Child's World®
childsworld.com

Published by The Child's World®
1980 Lookout Drive • Mankato, MN 56003-1705
800-599-READ • www.childsworld.com

ISBN 9781503819870
LCCN 2016961199

Printing
Printed in the United States of America
PA02334

Ann Heinrichs is the author of more than 100 books for children and young adults. She has also enjoyed successful careers as a children's book editor and an advertising copywriter. Ann grew up in Fort Smith, Arkansas, and lives in Chicago, Illinois.

About the Author
Ann Heinrichs

Matt Kania loves maps and, as a kid, dreamed of making them. In school he studied geography and cartography, and today he makes maps for a living. Matt's favorite thing about drawing maps is learning about the places they represent. Many of the maps he has created can be found in books, magazines, videos, Web sites, and public places.

About the
Map Illustrator
Matt Kania

On the cover: The Seattle skyline in Washington

OUR WASHINGTON TRIP

WASHINGTON

It's time for a trip through Washington! You'll have some great adventures there.

You'll climb mountains and hike through forests. You'll eat salmon roasted on a stick. You'll sail through the sky over a city. You'll watch gigantic whales leaping in the ocean.

That's a lot of activity, so don't wait. Just follow that loopy dotted line. You're in for lots of fun. Now, buckle up and let's hit the road!

WELCOME TO
WASHINGTON

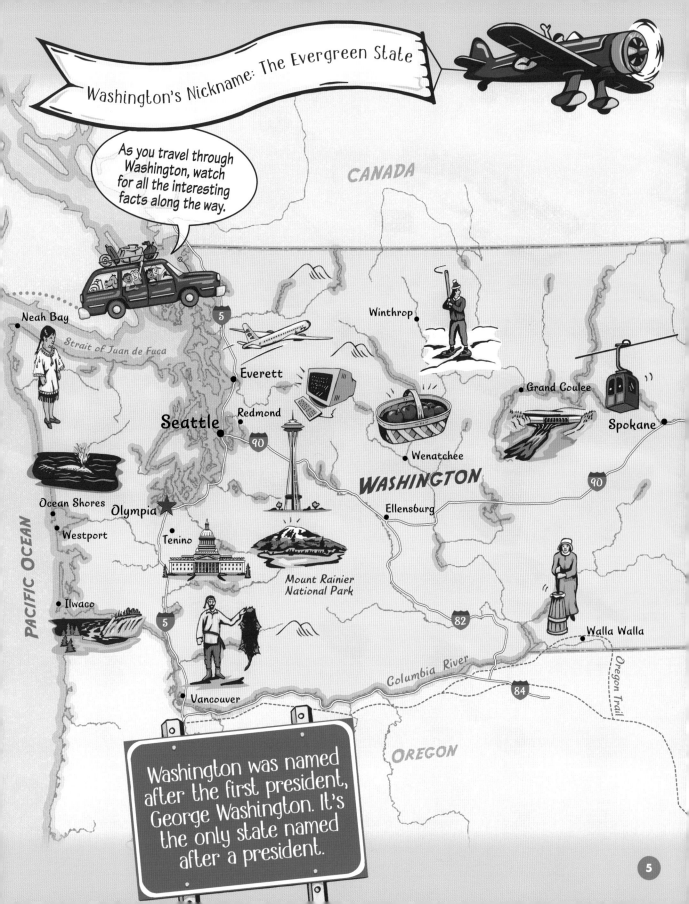

Washington's Nickname: The Evergreen State

As you travel through Washington, watch for all the interesting facts along the way.

CANADA

Neah Bay

Strait of Juan de Fuca

Winthrop

Grand Coulee

Spokane

Everett

Redmond

Seattle

Wenatchee

WASHINGTON

Ellensburg

Ocean Shores

Olympia

Westport

Tenino

Mount Rainier National Park

Ilwaco

Walla Walla

Columbia River

Vancouver

Oregon Trail

PACIFIC OCEAN

OREGON

Washington was named after the first president, George Washington. It's the only state named after a president.

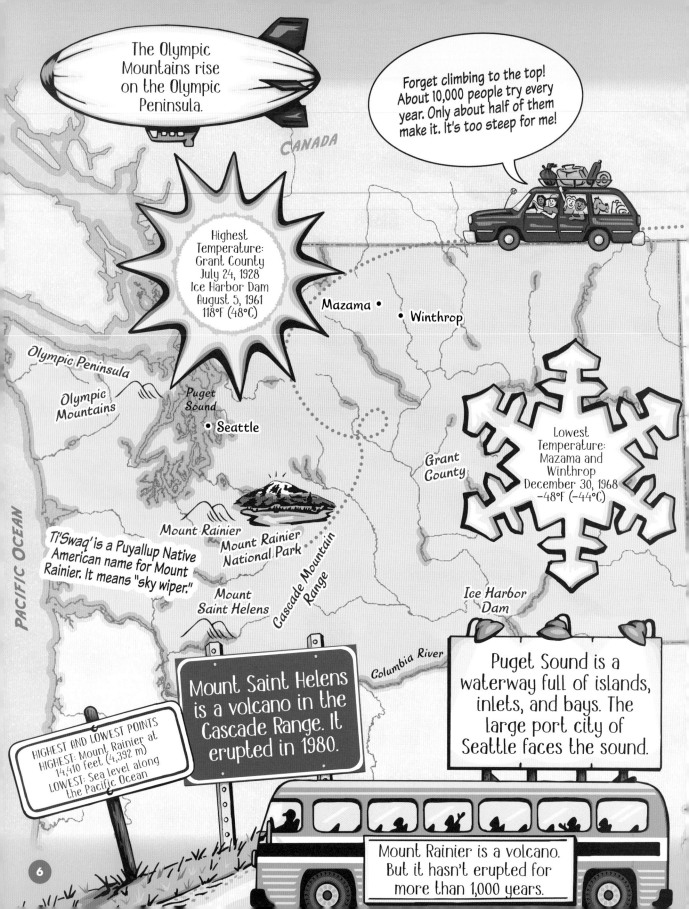

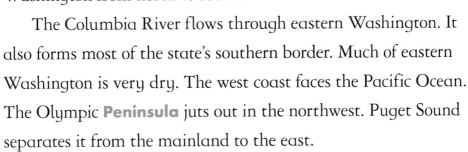

Hike along the mountain's edge. Or try climbing toward the peak. Maybe you'd like camping along a mountain stream. Or just lounging in a meadow of wildflowers. You're enjoying Mount Rainier National Park!

Snow-covered Mount Rainier is Washington's highest peak. It's part of the Cascade Mountain Range. The Cascades run through Washington from north to south.

The Columbia River flows through eastern Washington. It also forms most of the state's southern border. Much of eastern Washington is very dry. The west coast faces the Pacific Ocean. The Olympic **Peninsula** juts out in the northwest. Puget Sound separates it from the mainland to the east.

Mount Rainier is the tallest mountain in Washington.

WINTHROP'S SNOWSHOE SOFTBALL TOURNAMENT

How fast can you run? Try putting on some big old snowshoes. Then try running in the snow. You wouldn't be so fast, would you?

That's what people do in Winthrop. They hold the Snowshoe Softball Tournament every winter. Everyone runs the bases wearing snowshoes!

People in Washington have lots of winter fun. They ski on the snowy mountain slopes. Or they go ice-skating and snowmobiling. When it's warmer, they go hiking or boating. Mountain climbing is popular, too. Do you love the outdoors? Then Washington's the place for you!

Washington has many winter activities for visitors to enjoy.

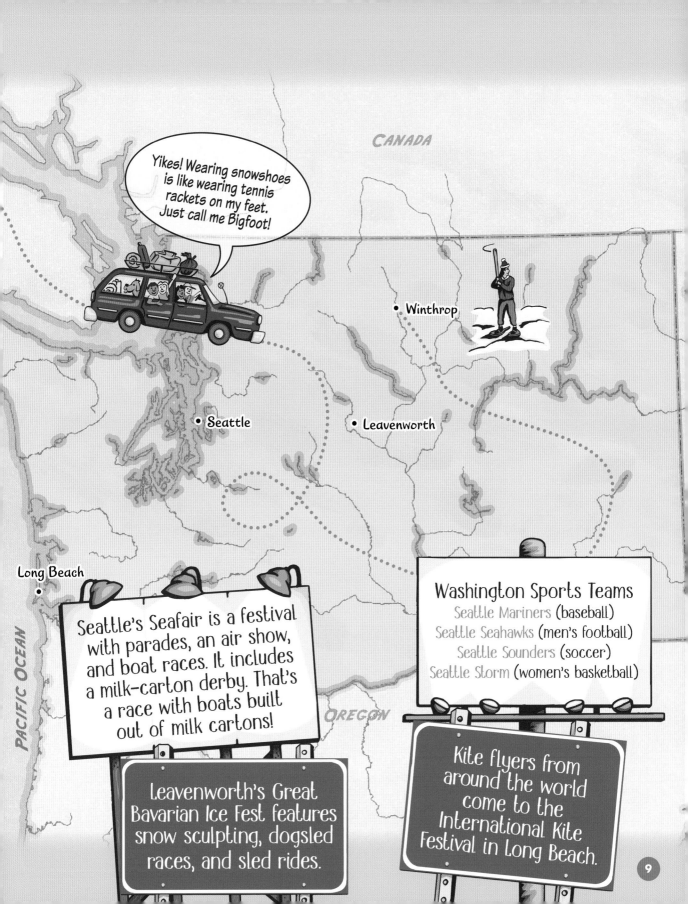

Baja California is part of the Mexico. It's just south of the state of California.

STATE FLOWER
COAST RHODODENDRON

STATE TREE
WESTERN HEMLOCK

STATE BIRD
WILLOW GOLDFINCH

CANADA

Rocky Mountains

Olympic Peninsula

Rain forests grow on the Olympic Peninsula. They're among the wettest places in the world.

Ocean Shores

Westport

Whoa! That whale is bigger than my school bus!

PACIFIC OCEAN

Salmon return to their birthplaces to breed. From the ocean, they swim upstream in the rivers. Several dams have fish ladders. These devices enable salmon to travel upstream.

OREGON

More than 20,000 gray whales migrate past Washington between March and May every year.

The National Park Service has 18 sites in Washington.

You probably know that birds **migrate**. But did you know that whales migrate, too? Gray whales have their babies near Baja California. Then they migrate north to the Arctic Ocean. Want to watch them? Just go to Westport or Ocean Shores!

Washington is home to many wild animals. Deer and elk live in the forested mountains. Mountain goats scamper on the rocky slopes. Overhead, you'll see graceful eagles and hawks. Ducks, herons, and other waterbirds inhabit the wetlands. The Rocky Mountains reach into northeastern Washington. There you'll find moose and even grizzly bears.

Gray whales swim approximately 12,430 miles (20,000 km) each year.

MAKAH DAYS FAIR IN NEAH BAY

Salmon is roasting on sticks around the fire. Eager paddlers take off for the canoe races. Soon the dances and fireworks will begin. You're attending Makah Days Fair in Neah Bay!

The Makah are one of Washington's Native American tribes. **Traditionally**, their ancestors made their living from the sea. They caught salmon, seals, and whales. Even children had small canoes. The Makah people lived in longhouses built of cedar.

The Makah Days Fair takes place in August. During this weekend-long event, members of the tribe celebrate their culture. Anyone is welcome to join in! Events include traditional dances, salmon bakes, and war canoe races.

Today, Washington has many Native American tribes. Some tribes include the Confederated Tribes of the Chehalis Reservation, the Cowlitz Indian Tribe, the Nisqually Indian Tribe, and the Upper Skagit Indian Tribe of Washington.

Try some freshly caught salmon at the Makah Days Fair.

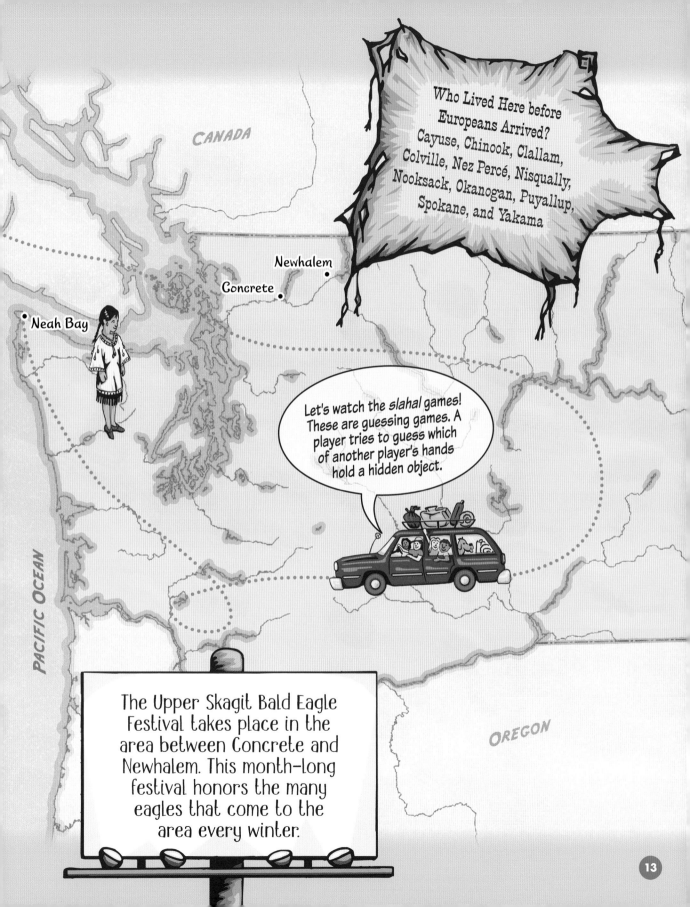

Who Lived Here before Europeans Arrived? Cayuse, Chinook, Clallam, Colville, Nez Percé, Nisqually, Nooksack, Okanogan, Puyallup, Spokane, and Yakama

CANADA

Newhalem

Concrete

Neah Bay

Let's watch the *slahal* games! These are guessing games. A player tries to guess which of another player's hands hold a hidden object.

PACIFIC OCEAN

OREGON

The Upper Skagit Bald Eagle Festival takes place in the area between Concrete and Newhalem. This month-long festival honors the many eagles that come to the area every winter.

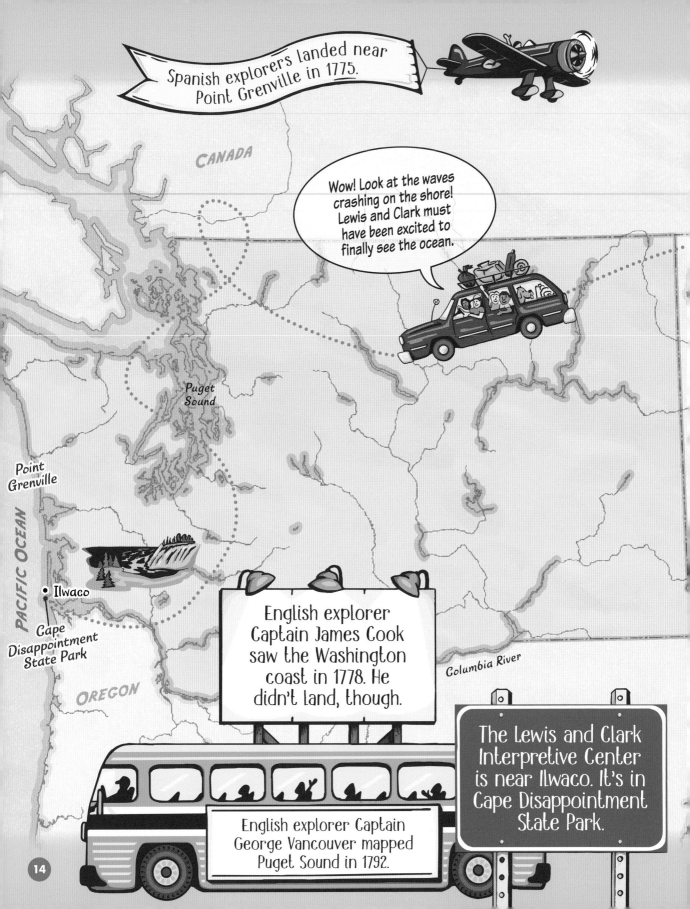

Spanish explorers landed near Point Grenville in 1775.

CANADA

Wow! Look at the waves crashing on the shore! Lewis and Clark must have been excited to finally see the ocean.

Puget Sound

Point Grenville

PACIFIC OCEAN

Ilwaco

Cape Disappointment State Park

OREGON

Columbia River

English explorer Captain James Cook saw the Washington coast in 1778. He didn't land, though.

The Lewis and Clark Interpretive Center is near Ilwaco. It's in Cape Disappointment State Park.

English explorer Captain George Vancouver mapped Puget Sound in 1792.

Many years ago, traders wanted Washington's valuable fur-bearing animals. They had heard of a great river here, too. It emptied into the Pacific Ocean.

English fur trader John Meares sailed by in 1788. But he found no river. So he named a rocky point Cape Disappointment. U.S. fur trader Robert Gray was luckier. He found the river in 1792. He named it the Columbia River. Then the United States claimed the region.

Explorers Meriwether Lewis and William Clark traveled cross-country. Following the Columbia River, they arrived at Cape Disappointment. But they were not disappointed. They reached the Pacific Ocean in 1805. Just visit Cape Disappointment. You'll learn all about their trip!

The North Head Lighthouse overlooks Cape Disappointment.

FORT VANCOUVER NATIONAL HISTORIC SITE

Smell delicious food cooked on wood-burning stoves. Hear the carpenter hammering away. Watch the blacksmith pounding metal into tools. You're at Fort Vancouver National Historic Site! It used to be a fur-trading post. You can watch its old-time activities every summer.

Fur traders had many trading posts in Washington. People from the United States and Great Britain built them. Both nations were trying to control the region.

A British company built Fort Vancouver in 1825. Hundreds of people worked there. Many were trappers who ventured into the wilderness. Others worked in the nearby village. They grew crops and built ships. They supplied whatever the fort needed.

Fort Vancouver burned down in 1866. But the fort has been rebuilt for modern-day visitors.

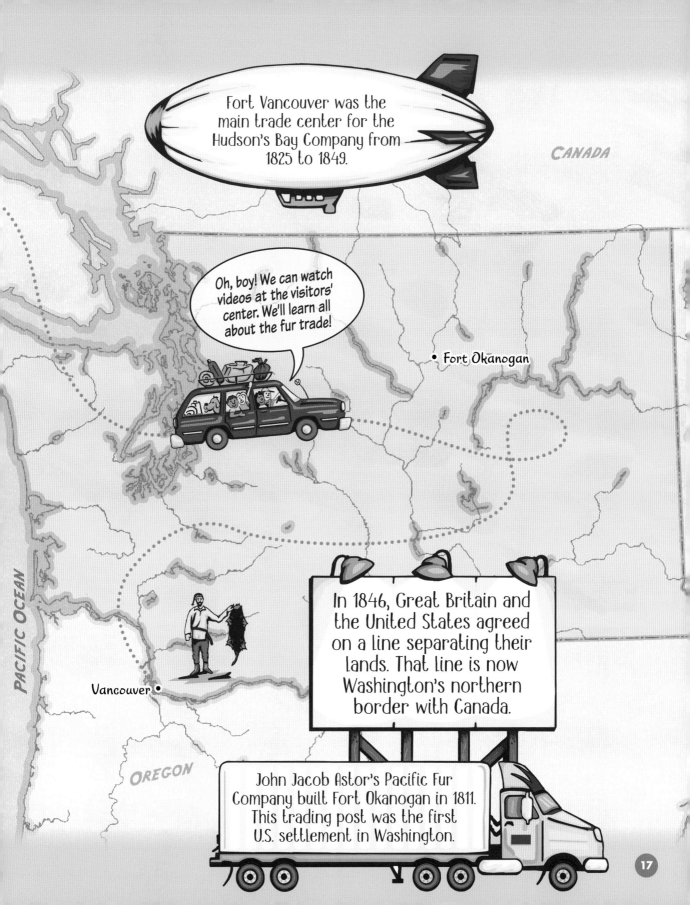

Fort Vancouver was the main trade center for the Hudson's Bay Company from 1825 to 1849.

CANADA

Oh, boy! We can watch videos at the visitors' center. We'll learn all about the fur trade!

Fort Okanogan

PACIFIC OCEAN

In 1846, Great Britain and the United States agreed on a line separating their lands. That line is now Washington's northern border with Canada.

Vancouver

OREGON

John Jacob Astor's Pacific Fur Company built Fort Okanogan in 1811. This trading post was the first U.S. settlement in Washington.

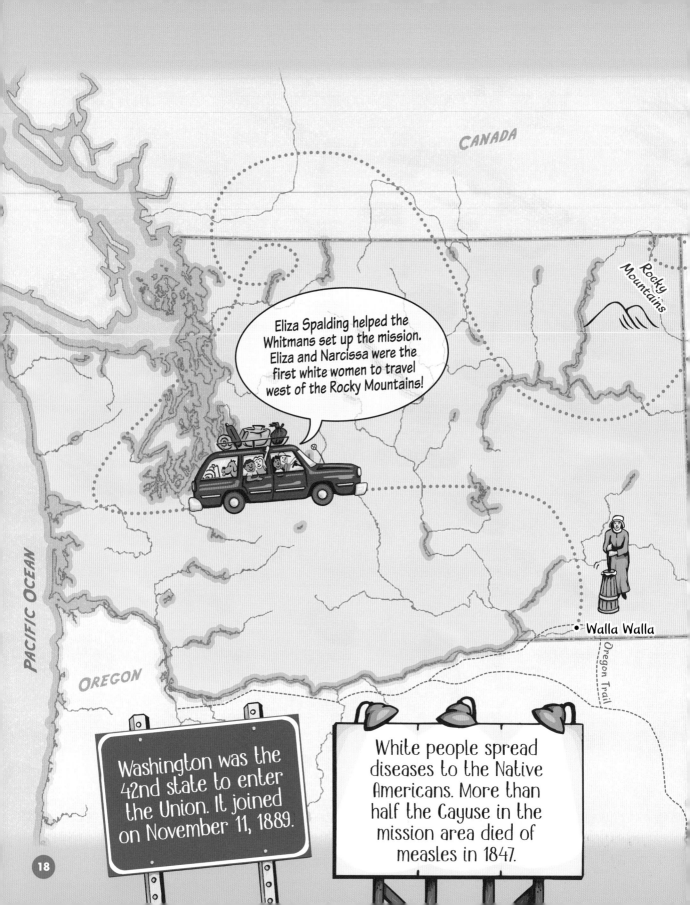

WHITMAN MISSION NEAR WALLA WALLA

Try churning some butter. It's hard work! Then try making some adobe bricks. You make them with clay and straw. You're enjoying a summer weekend at Whitman **Mission**. It's a national historic site near Walla Walla.

Marcus and Narcissa Whitman once lived here. They opened a mission for Cayuse Native Americans in 1836. They wanted to teach their religion to the Native Americans and change their way of life. Many **pioneers** stopped by, too. They were following the Oregon Trail. They had traveled far in covered wagons. They hoped to build farms in the West.

The Whitman Mission has lots of information about the history of the Oregon Trail. The park also has many trails to explore.

Visitors to the Whitman Mission can view a replica wagon travelers used on the Oregon Trail.

THE STATE CAPITOL IN OLYMPIA

Washington's capitol is a **symbol** of strength. It's also just plain strong! An earthquake struck in 2001. The dome cracked, and ten columns moved. Today, the restored building stands secure.

The capitol in Olympia is the center of state government. Washington has three branches of government. One branch makes the state laws. Its members meet in the capitol. The governor heads another branch. Its job is to carry out the laws. Judges make up the third branch. They listen to cases in courts. Then they decide whether laws have been broken.

Washington's capitol dome rises 175 feet (53 m) above the floor.

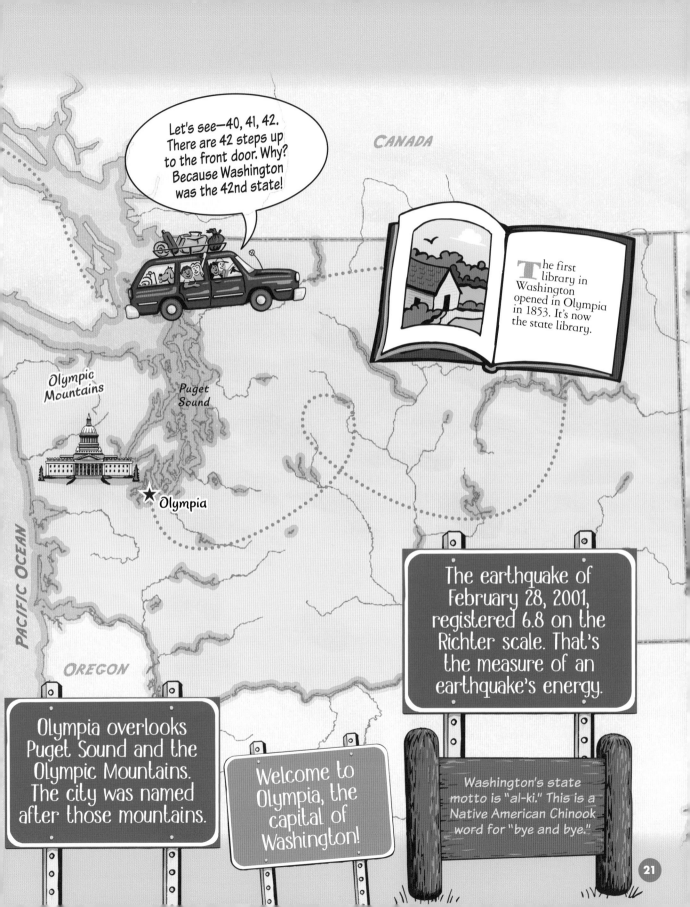

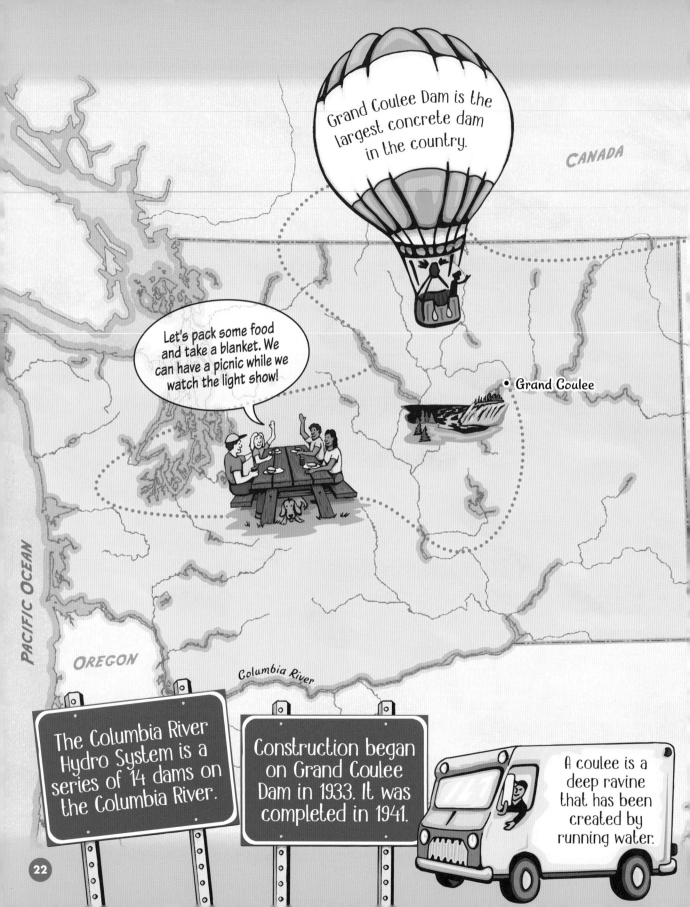

Grand Coulee Dam is the largest concrete dam in the country.

CANADA

Let's pack some food and take a blanket. We can have a picnic while we watch the light show!

• Grand Coulee

PACIFIC OCEAN

OREGON

Columbia River

The Columbia River Hydro System is a series of 14 dams on the Columbia River.

Construction began on Grand Coulee Dam in 1933. It was completed in 1941.

A coulee is a deep ravine that has been created by running water.

Take a shuttle right down to the face of the dam. At the bottom, there's a massive power plant. It creates electricity for homes miles away. But the best part comes after dark. You'll watch a spectacular light show. It dances across the wall of the dam! It occurs from Memorial Day to the end of September.

You're exploring the Grand Coulee Dam near the town of Grand Coulee. Washington workers began building large dams in the 1930s. The dams do a lot for the state. They direct water into farmers' fields. They also control floods and produce electric power.

Grand Coulee Dam provides water for about 600,000 acres (243,000 ha) of land.

APPLE BLOSSOM FESTIVAL

Hop on the carnival rides. Join the golf tournament. Eat apples at the Food Fair. You're at the Washington State Apple Blossom Festival in Wenatchee! The festival takes place from the end of April to the beginning of May. Thousands of people come to this festival. It's known as the oldest festival in Washington!

This festival celebrates Washington's favorite fruit. No other state grows more apples than Washington. And no state grows more pears, either. Washington also grows a lot of wheat. Much of it grows in eastern Washington.

Much of eastern Washington is naturally dry. But farms in its river valleys are very fertile. That's because **irrigation** brings water to the fields. Many farmers raise cattle for beef and milk. Trees are valuable products, too.

Washington's apple harvest starts in August and ends in November.

The Green Bluff Apple Festival is held in Spokane from September to October.

CANADA

What Are Washington's Fishing Products?
Salmon, albacore, herring, rockfish, and cod

Let's join the other kids for Youth Day! It's a part of the Apple Blossom Festival. We can get our faces painted and play games!

Monroe

Spokane •

Wenatchee •

Puyallup •

Grayland •

PACIFIC OCEAN

Washington's southwest coast is called the Cranberry Coast. Grayland and Long Beach hold cranberry festivals in October.

Yakima •

Long Beach •

There are three state fairs in Washington each year. The Washington State Fair in Puyallup is in September. The Central Washington State Fair is in Yakima in late September, and the Evergreen State Fair is in Monroe in late August.

OREGON

What Does Washington Raise?
Apples, milk, wheat, potatoes, beef cattle, hay, cherries, grapes, and pears

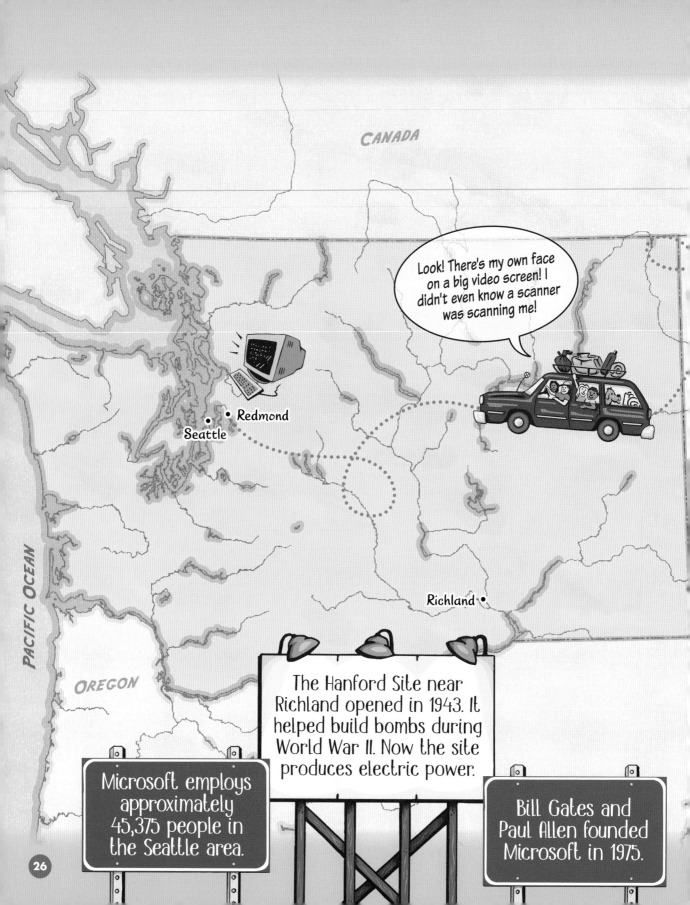

THE MICROSOFT VISITOR CENTER IN REDMOND

Make a movie and star in it, too. Try your luck at the latest computer games. See the first personal computer ever made. Discover what the future holds for computers. You're exploring the Microsoft Visitor Center in Redmond!

Microsoft is one of Washington's biggest companies. It sells its products all over the world.

Washington was busy during World War II (1939–1945). It made military aircraft and ships. Its farms also supplied food for the troops.

Many new **industries** grew after the war. One is the Boeing aircraft company. And, of course, there's Microsoft!

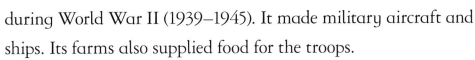

Stop by Microsoft's main campus in Redmond.

EVERETT'S BOEING FACTORY

Have you ever built a model airplane? Your project probably covered a desk or table. Now imagine building a full-size airplane. You need lots of room for that. Just visit the Boeing factory in Everett. It's the world's largest building by volume! There you'll see massive airplane parts. And you'll learn how they're put together.

Boeing is the world's largest aircraft maker. Transportation equipment is Washington's top factory product. Shipbuilding is another big industry. Computer products are also important. Washington produces many foods and wood products, too.

More than 3,000 airplanes have been built at Boeing's factory in Everett.

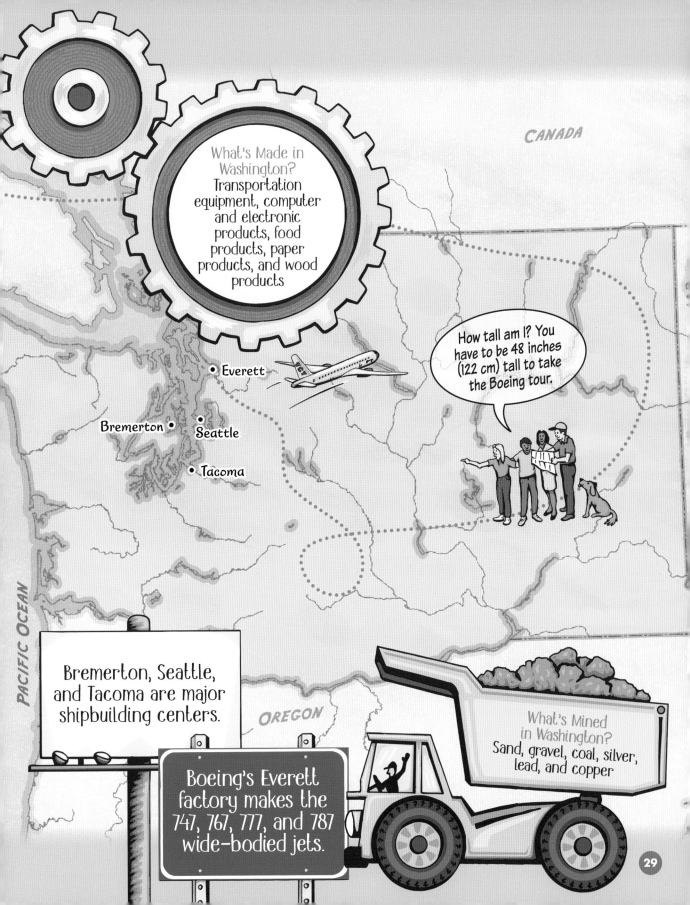

What's Made in Washington? Transportation equipment, computer and electronic products, food products, paper products, and wood products

CANADA

How tall am I? You have to be 48 inches (122 cm) tall to take the Boeing tour.

Everett

Bremerton   Seattle

Tacoma

PACIFIC OCEAN

Bremerton, Seattle, and Tacoma are major shipbuilding centers.

OREGON

What's Mined in Washington? Sand, gravel, coal, silver, lead, and copper

Boeing's Everett factory makes the 747, 767, 777, and 787 wide-bodied jets.

In 2016, 7,288,000 people lived in Washington. It's the 13th-largest state by population.

Let's take the Seattle Underground Tour! We'll visit old buildings that sank into the ground!

CANADA

The Museum of Flight in Seattle has exhibits on the history of aviation.

Puget Sound

• Seattle

• Tacoma

Spokane •

PACIFIC OCEAN

OREGON

Seattle held the Century 21 Exposition, a world's fair, in 1962. The city built its Space Needle for the occasion.

Seattle's Museum of Pop Culture is a rock-and-roll museum.

POPULATION OF LARGEST CITIES
Seattle..........................684,451
Spokane........................213,272
Tacoma.........................207,948

More than half of Washington's residents live in the Puget Sound Region.

EXPLORING SEATTLE

Seattle is a great place to explore. Its tall, pointy Space Needle towers over the city. From the top, you can see for miles. Nearby is the Pacific Science Center. You'll see life-size moving dinosaurs there. Things are moving at the Seattle Aquarium, too. They include otters and octopuses!

Many **immigrants** settled in Seattle. It became Washington's biggest city. It's a major shipping center for Asian trade.

Check out Seattle's Northwest Folklife Festival. You'll eat Greek, Thai, and African foods there. You'll hear the music of Mexico, Scotland, and Japan. And you'll see dances from many Asian lands. All these **ethnic** groups made Washington their home.

The Space Needle is 605 feet (184 m) tall.

RIDING IN STYLE IN SPOKANE

Spokane is a fun place to visit. It has some unusual rides. One is the **carousel** in Riverfront Park. It has 54 beautifully decorated horses. Their tails are made from real horse hair. There's a giraffe and a tiger, too. Or maybe you'd prefer the Chinese dragon chairs!

Are you tired of riding in circles? Then take the Gondola SkyRide. It moves along wires high in the sky. You get on the gondola in Riverfront Park. Then you go soaring high above the city. Look down and see the thundering Spokane Falls. Whee!

The Red Wagon statue in Riverfront Park can hold up to 300 people!

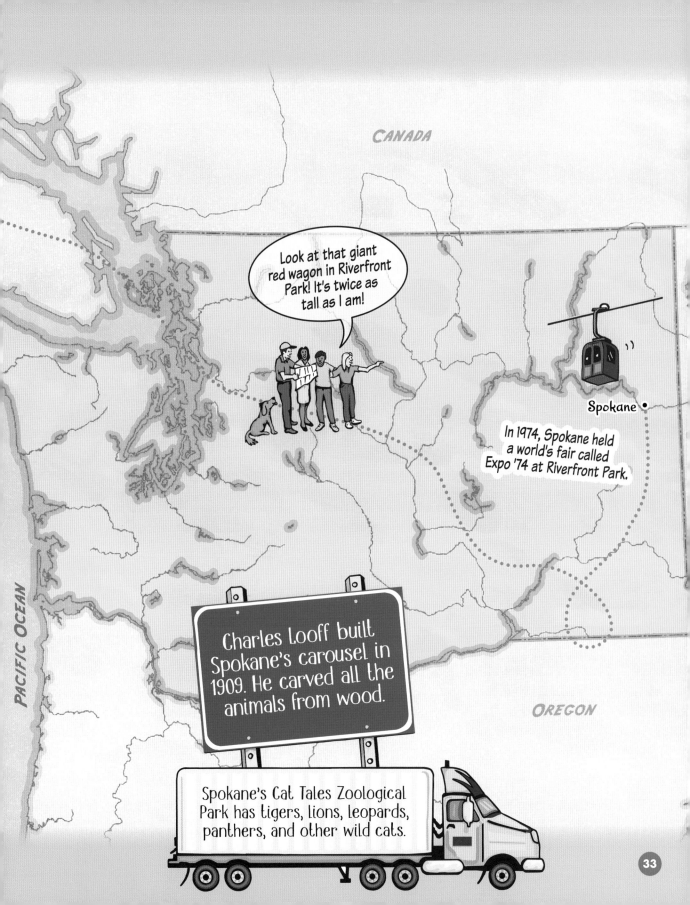

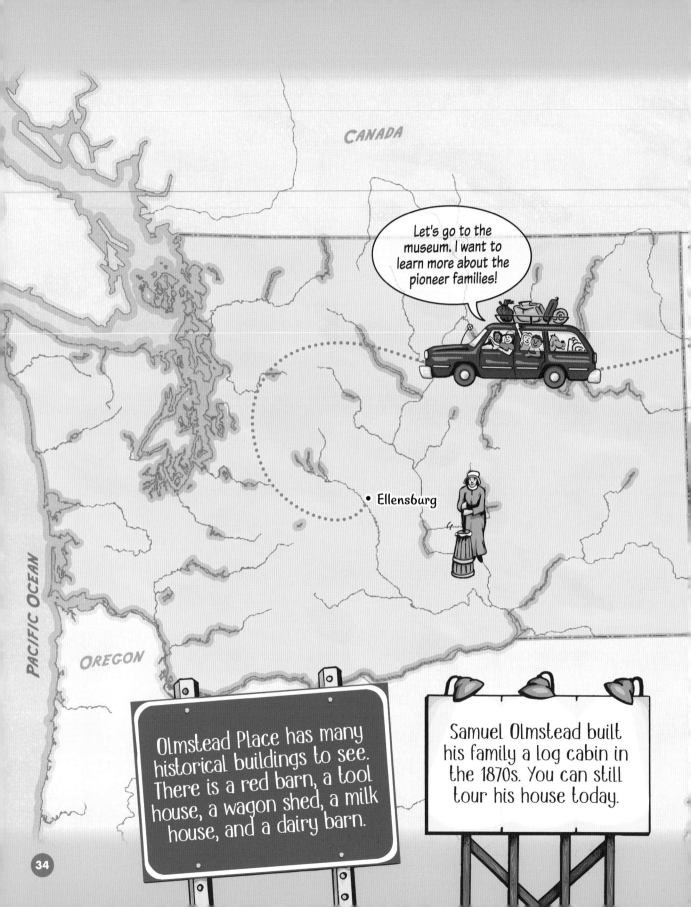

CANADA

Let's go to the museum. I want to learn more about the pioneer families!

• Ellensburg

PACIFIC OCEAN

OREGON

Olmstead Place has many historical buildings to see. There is a red barn, a tool house, a wagon shed, a milk house, and a dairy barn.

Samuel Olmstead built his family a log cabin in the 1870s. You can still tour his house today.

OLMSTEAD PLACE IN ELLENSBURG

Are you interested in learning about pioneer life? Then take a visit to the Olmstead Place Historical State Park in Ellensburg!

This park has 217 acres (88 ha) of land. Visitors can walk through historic gardens and tour a log cabin. Pioneers' belongings are on display, too. You can see tools, clothing, furniture, machinery, and household items.

When you're done touring the house, step outside and enjoy the hiking trails! Bring your fishing pole, because you can fish in the park. In the winter visitors can go snowshoeing and cross-country skiing.

Visitors can receive free guided tours of Olmstead Place on weekends.

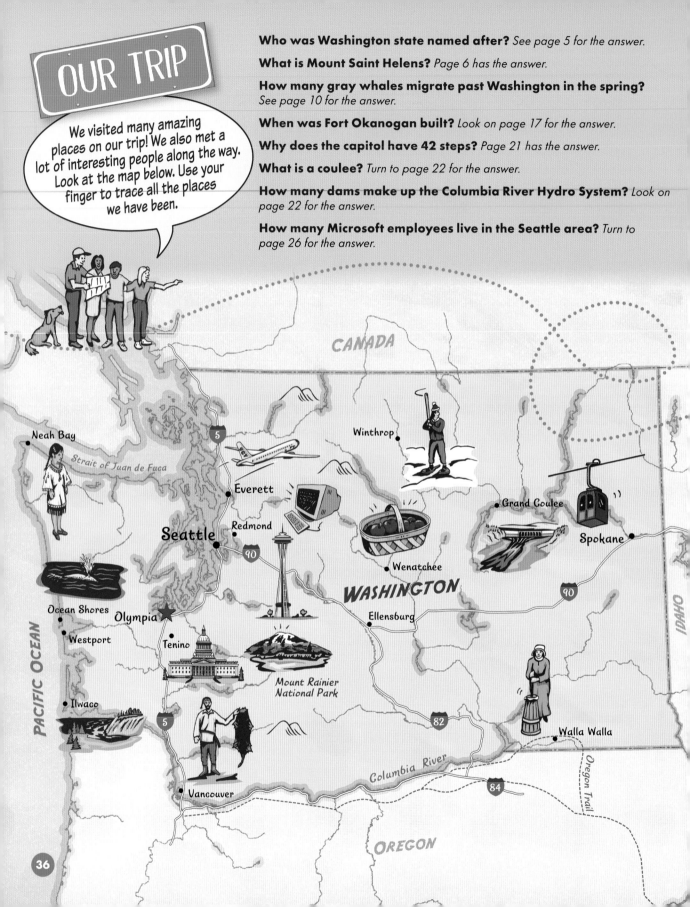

OUR TRIP

We visited many amazing places on our trip! We also met a lot of interesting people along the way. Look at the map below. Use your finger to trace all the places we have been.

Who was Washington state named after? *See page 5 for the answer.*

What is Mount Saint Helens? *Page 6 has the answer.*

How many gray whales migrate past Washington in the spring? *See page 10 for the answer.*

When was Fort Okanogan built? *Look on page 17 for the answer.*

Why does the capitol have 42 steps? *Page 21 has the answer.*

What is a coulee? *Turn to page 22 for the answer.*

How many dams make up the Columbia River Hydro System? *Look on page 22 for the answer.*

How many Microsoft employees live in the Seattle area? *Turn to page 26 for the answer.*

CANADA

Neah Bay

Strait of Juan de Fuca

Winthrop

Everett

Grand Coulee

Seattle

Redmond

Spokane

WASHINGTON

Wenatchee

Ocean Shores

Olympia

Ellensburg

Westport

Tenino

Mount Rainier National Park

Walla Walla

Ilwaco

PACIFIC OCEAN

IDAHO

Columbia River

Vancouver

Oregon Trail

OREGON

STATE SYMBOLS

State bird: Willow goldfinch

State dance: Square dance

State fish: Steelhead trout

State flower: Coast rhododendron

State folk song: "Roll On, Columbia, Roll On"

State fossil: Columbian mammoth

State fruit: Apple

State gem: Petrified wood

State grass: Bluebunch wheatgrass

State insect: Green darner dragonfly

State ship: *Lady Washington*

State tree: Western hemlock

STATE SONG

"WASHINGTON, MY HOME"
Words and music by Helen Davis

This is my country; God gave it to me;
I will protect it, ever keep it free.
Small towns and cities rest here in the sun,
Filled with our laughter, "Thy will be done."

Washington, my home;
Where ever I may roam;
This is my land, my native land,
Washington, my home.
Our verdant forest green,
Caressed by silvery stream.

From mountain peak to fields of wheat,
Washington, my home.

There's peace you feel and understand
In this, our own beloved land.
We greet the day with head held high,
And forward ever is our cry.
We'll happy ever be
As people always free.
For you and me a destiny;
Washington my home.

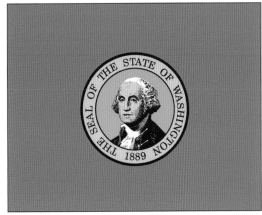

State flag

That was a great trip! We have traveled all over Washington. There are a few places that we didn't have time for, though. Next time, we plan to visit Wolf Haven in Tenino. Visitors can view wolves, foxes, and coyotes. They learn how wolves live in the wild and why it's important to protect them.

State seal

FAMOUS PEOPLE

Boeing, William (1881-1956), aircraft manufacturer

Carlson, Chester F. (1906-1968), inventor

Chihuly, Dale (1941-), glass artist

Crosby, Bing (1903-1977), singer and actor

Crutcher, Chris (1946-), children's author

Cunningham, Merce (1919-2009), choreographer

Gates, Bill (1955-), billionaire who helped create Microsoft

Haggerty, Benjamin "Macklemore" (1983-), singer

Herbert, Frank (1920-1986), novelist

Jones, Chuck (1912-2002), animator who helped create the Bugs Bunny cartoons

Kehret, Peg (1936-), children's author

Kenny G (1956-), musician

LaVine, Zach (1995-), basketball player

Lewis, Ryan (1988-), musician, record producer, and recording artist

Morgan, Jeffrey Dean (1966-), actor

Ohno, Apolo Anton (1982-), speed skater and Olympic medalist

Rashad, Ahmad (1949-), sportscaster

Sandberg, Ryne (1959-), baseball player

Scobee, Francis (1939-1986), astronaut

Seattle (1786-1866), Native American chief of the Wallowa band of the Nez Percé

Smohalla (1820-1895), Wanapum Native American and religious leader

West, Adam (1928-), actor

Wilson, August (1945-2005), playwright

WORDS TO KNOW

carousel (kar-uh-SELL) a merry-go-round

ethnic (ETH-nik) relating to a person's race or nationality

immigrants (IM-uh-gruhnts) people who move to another country

industries (IN-duh-streez) types of business

irrigation (ihr-uh-GAY-shuhn) a method of bringing water to fields through ditches or pipes

migrate (MY-grate) to move from location to location, often following the seasons

mission (MISH-uhn) a place where people try to spread their religion

peninsula (puh-NIN-soo-lah) a piece of land almost completely surrounded by water

pioneers (pye-uh-NEERZ) people who move into an area unsettled by Europeans

symbol (SIMM-bull) something that stands for an idea or value

traditionally (truh-DISH-uh-nul-lee) following long-held customs

TO LEARN MORE

IN THE LIBRARY

Demuth, Patricia Brennan. *Who Is Bill Gates?* New York, NY: Grosset & Dunlap, 2013.

St. George, Judith. *What Was the Lewis and Clark Expedition?* New York, NY: Grosset & Dunlap, 2014.

Winters, Kay. *Voices from the Oregon Trail*. New York, NY: Dial Books for Young Readers, 2014.

ON THE WEB

Visit our Web site for links about Washington:

childsworld.com/links

Note to Parents, Teachers, and Librarians: We routinely verify our Web links to make sure they are safe and active sites. So encourage your readers to check them out!

PLACES TO VISIT OR CONTACT

Washington State History Museum

washingtonhistory.org
1911 Pacific Avenue
Tacoma, WA 98402
253/272-9747
For more information about the history of Washington

Washington the State

experiencewa.com
P.O. Box 953
Seattle, WA 98111
800/544-1800
For more information about traveling in Washington

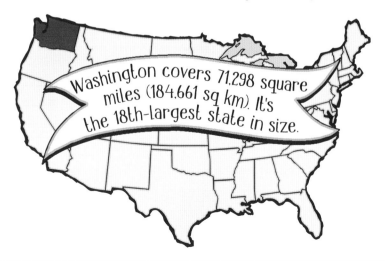

Washington covers 71,298 square miles (184,661 sq km). It's the 18th-largest state in size.

INDEX

Bye, Evergreen State. We had a great time. We'll come back soon!